Close Enough

poems by

Mike Dillon

Finishing Line Press
Georgetown, Kentucky

Close Enough

Copyright © 2023 by Mike Dillon
ISBN 979-8-88838-314-8 First Edition
All rights reserved under International and Pan-American Copyright Conventions. No part of this book may be reproduced in any manner whatsoever without written permission from the publisher, except in the case of brief quotations embodied in critical articles and reviews.

ACKNOWLEDGMENTS

The following poems, some since revised, first appeared in these publications:

Childhood Forest: *Off the Coast*
World War II: *Eunoia Review*
April 10, 1963; Vietnam; *Masque & Spectacle*
Village in Southern France: *Dappled Things*
Then: *Bellowing Ark*
At My Father's Old Battlefield, Jebsheim, France: *Prometheus Dreaming*
In May: *Rue Scribe*
Nocturne: *Bellowing Ark*
Holocaust Denier: *Take a Stand: Art Against Hate*
A Small Thing: *Current*
Consider; At Last, the Sea: *Galway Review* (Ireland)
Patriot: *Poetry Salzburg Review* (Austria)

Publisher: Leah Huete de Maines
Editor: Christen Kincaid
Cover Art: Sydni Sterling
Author Photo: Sydni Sterling
Cover Design: Elizabeth Maines McCleavy

Order online: www.finishinglinepress.com
      also available on amazon.com

Author inquiries and mail orders:
Finishing Line Press
PO Box 1626
Georgetown, Kentucky 40324
USA

Table of Contents

Kyoto 1

Photograph in August, Age Five 2

Childhood Forest 3

April 10, 1963 4

World War II 5

Vietnam 6

Estuary 7

Village in Southern France 8

Then 9

At My Father's Old Battlefield 10

In May 11

Nocturne 12

Out of the Woods 13

Close Enough 14

Pre-Posthumous 15

Patriot 16

Holocaust Denier 17

Small Thing 18

Family Reunion Picnic 19

At Last, the Sea 20

Consider 21

To Thomas Patrick Haley
1942-2011

No friendship is an accident. —O. Henry

Kyoto

*Who among us has not grown to consider
 what real loss is?*

*Not loss of grandparents,
 (a grief-cape waved at a bull bearing a padded horn)*

*or even loss of parents (the horn-pierced heart
 still beats),*

*but to wonder if we've settled for less
 than the world was ready to give,*

*or to feel, as Basho did,
 even if it's only for one breath-beat,*

*what it means to stand in the heart of Kyoto
 longing for Kyoto.*

Photograph in August, Age Five

A sweet gaze locked into the camera's gaze—
still innocent with the shock
of incarnation.

1955: memories forever fixed in black and white.
Even so, I know the stripes on his t-shirt are blue
as the saliva-warm lake behind him.

One day such innocence will grow up to write:
"Just by walking I waded in deep.
And the waters closed over my head."

An underwater forest of too many years
stands between here and there,
though he will find, along the way,

sunlit clearings, green silence of moss,
the quicksilver vocables of a nameless stream.
And a day will come when he will stop to hear

an unknown bird's liquid carol
along his penumbral path winding
back towards the source of light.

Patience, dear boy.
The path will find its way here
where, at last, I can help you.

Childhood Forest

Far away but close enough to hear my mother's call
I sat in my secret, sunlit place of cedar and salal
in that antebellum year before kindergarten
when my gray, short-haired cat emerged from the brush
with a squirrel clamped in his jaws
to stroll right past me with a lunar stare
into nothingness as the squirrel's mouth
   dripped blood-red berries.

My hushed, urgent calls to my pal,
my bedmate, my friend, did not slow him
from sifting back into the brush
with an indifference that scalded my skin
in a world I had thought secretly loved me
that left me deeper in the woods that I'd been
with those blood-red berries
   shining in the sun.

April 10, 1963

I first heard the word "Jew" said in that certain way at my grandmother's house on April 10, 1963 when I was twelve.

I know the exact date because on the short drive to my grandmother's my mother had the radio on, and there came a news bulletin with a man saying the nuclear submarine Thresher has vanished a few hundred miles east of Boston.

We soon arrived at my grandmother's. She was just back from her first winter in Florida with her second husband, a retired U.S. Navy officer who believed he never got the high rank he felt he deserved.

From the next room I paged through a *National Geographic* with polar ice and African breasts, but I was really listening to their talk about Florida—the palm trees and warm ocean water.

And then my grandmother's second husband compound-fractured the day: "The damn Jews were everywhere." Then came my mother's conspiratorial "Shhh!" in the way one adult shushes another because tender ears are nearby.

Goosebumps, and a sudden chill, reminded me of the flesh I wore.

I'd read Anne Frank in school. The good guys, my dad included, had won the War. They couldn't save Anne Frank but they saved the rest of the world. I thought the crow-black shadows had been chased away forever. I thought there would be no more Anne Franks.

On the drive home, the radio off, I didn't say much. The world out the window lay like a sheeted corpse beneath the soft, late afternoon sunlight of April.

I already knew the Thresher had sunk.

World War II

The war my father never spoke of
lived in the sixth-grade history book
I lugged home from school.
On the school bus
my book enclosed a flame.
I looked around to make sure
the other kids hadn't noticed.
Everything was the same:
all shoulder punches and guffaws
thrashing in that liminal zone
between childhood and horse laughs.
Some nights, at the dinner table for five,
I'd sneak a studious peak at my father's
sky-blue eyes flecked with arctic cold.
I wanted to know what lay behind them.
I wanted to know what it was like
to have been inside the book I carried home.
I wondered how much of the world
would be shut out from me,
forever unknowable and strange.
And if flames would ever lick up
through the floorboards of my own life.

Vietnam

A couple of years after high school he came home from Vietnam in a coffin.

A doughy, overweight boy who played no sports, joined no clubs. He nodded off in class instead. His family lived in an old, dingy house on a few tattered acres with their chickens and hogs.

(The place is a manicured gentleman's farm now, with the requisite llama and a pair of golden retrievers).

"I'm sleeping so I don't get tired," he informed one white-knuckled teacher to a squall of teen-aged laughter.

One morning at the school bus stop—this must have been 1965—he made a running start at the frozen pond and ass-skidded all the way to the other side, accompanied by howls and cheers. He rose in exaggerated slow-motion, made a harlequin bow and doffed an imaginary top hat. He stood there, soaking it all up, the white plumes of his breath vanishing beneath the risen sun.

The school bus neared. The brakes scritched. The yellow door buckled open. And we all boarded for the same destination.

For a little while longer.

Estuary

The path through the woods takes a mile
before it breaks open to the full-tide pond
where rainbow trout and rock crabs abide
beneath a sky-blue sheen of fresh and salt water.

A picket line of dead firs borders the western edge.
A sandpiper's calligraphy inscribes the mud.
A round hole into the brush declares a fox trail.
A dead branch is kingfisher's Napoleonic perch.

And a rotted dory's blanched ribs,
like a stag abandoned by a discovered poacher,
settle year by year into the sedge
ticking in the soft breeze.

From the thicket of steel and glass towers
a dozen miles southeast across Puget Sound
comes the customary, lathe-like thrum.
You turn your back on the city.

A baroque white cloud drifts north.
A Nootka rose cups the last globule
of last night's rain, translucent in the sun.
And it is lovely. From any angle. It is lovely.

A Village in Southern France

...the trip is worth it only if the river's source is flowing.
—from a well-known guidebook

Upon dusty river-rock
mottled shade from a plane tree
flickers with water's fluency.

Upstream the famous fountain is dry.
This lyrical tableau of shade and stone
is not what tourists come for.

So, you wait with the others
for the tour bus to pull up
and point for better things.

The bus is late. Across the lane
there's a small stone chapel:
disused, scabrous,

a ninth century footnote to the town.
You open the oak door
and step into the darkness.

A few apertures of light reveal
a bare stone altar,
a worn keeling place.

Light that carries
an unbroken thread.
As it was. And is.

Then

A suave, blue river, silver-shot by a breeze
combed a tall, golden field
and stirred the lindens.

An empty rail station. An overdue train
on an empty Austrian Sunday in August.
I had dreamed it would be like this—

cottony clouds adrift in a river,
each of my breaths a sip of lost wine
from a future already ripened with patience.

And the winnowing angels had left me my dreams
with a shock-proof nave deep inside
where I prayed, sometimes, it would come true—

Goethe's poems on the table, a mullioned window
framing forest green, a trellis of pink roses, and the soft rain
you came in from to let down your long dark hair.

I shouldered my pack. Let the late train be.
I walked beside the river and you walked beside me.
Even then, I knew you existed.

At My Father's Old Battlefield: Jebsheim, France

My father never talked
about the War.

Sometimes the steep silence
   of an abandoned well
   swallowed him

and his blue eyes stared off
   into nowhere's
   somewhere.

An hour after his funeral my mother
  said to me
    he cried just once
    in his sleep
    and not like a little boy, either.

In May

Purple wisteria
and a red rhododendron
color a lush green world
in thin afternoon rain.

A brown horse steps
over the far field
with the slow fluency
of a mind at peace.

Rain patters the new leaves.
Rain falls through an archaic memory
not your own. Someone you
would recognize stood here
in another century.

And will again.

Nocturne

Lilacs fade to blue-shadowed scent.
Robin carols dwindle, one by one.
The first star has come to the garden.

Someday, maybe, God will fulfill his promise
and drain Narcissus's pond.
Someday, maybe, life will be as it is now,
simple as a children's story or old hymn.

Raucous laughter builds and bursts
from the near-stranger's house
you slipped out of into the deepening dusk.

White clematis stars the laurel hedge.
The second star has come to the garden.
Another round of their shouts and laughter
carbonates into spume.

You haven't drowned, despite your awkward evasions.
You stand here, quiet as moss—your own shore
in the shoreless flood.

Somewhere, out there, is a white path
found only in the dark. Remember:
the garden gate that let you in also opens out
into the sweet bowl of evening.

Out of the Woods

Before they met
loneliness filled their lives,
a loneliness that rhymed
with the heron's broken-branch cry
in a midnight wood.
Such a loneliness lacked
even solitude.

He'd come to fear
his life was a furled sail
in the world's eyes,
a fear that made him spin tropical tale after tale
into an azure nimbus around her soul.
Yet her olive-dark eyes never wavered from his.
Why, he still doesn't know.

And so
Eros and Thanatos two-stepped beneath the sun
and bucked up each other's awkward dance
as they stumbled toward a warm, blue ocean
beneath a sky teetering black and blue
to roll a pair of stolen dice
on their fairy tale of bliss. And it came up true.

Close Enough

> *I hold this to be the highest task of a bond between two people:*
> *that each should stand guard over the solitude of the other.*
> —*Rilke*

Close, let's not come closer.
There. Close enough.

To keep it like this—
our two-step to the music

only we can hear. Close enough to warm
myself beside your beauty.

Close enough that I may give you
everything you need.

And far apart enough we may never utter
"I know what you're thinking"

across the hairline crack between us—
our precious, rose-petalled moat.

Pre-Posthumous

I've known him all my life.
That's what they'll say
when mine is over.

What they knew about me
was my portable privet hedge
that kept them from knowing.

And those few, chosen confidences
that let them inch closer—
strategic tweaks to toss them off the trail.

Maybe you, too, have lingered
with a blue flower moving in the wind
after everyone else has moved on.

Or paused to gaze down upon the evening star
holding steady in an April-flooded ditch
after you quit the party early.

Patriot

The country inside is quiet as moss.
Everyone knows there's no money in moss.

A dun little bird just in from the mountains
brought with it the private right to be.

What might I stand up for?
Maybe just that.

Holocaust Denier

As he spoke
to scattered inattention
in the park when I walked past
the faceted interiors
of his green-eyed glance
locked into mine.

And I thought of my cat
hunched on the windowsill
that very morning
fused to a towhee flitting
in the laurel on the other side
of the glass.

Puffed cheeks, a guttural chortle.
The green seas of her eyes
dilated black as the spaces
between the stars that frightened
Pascal. I gave her a poke.
She didn't know me.

Small Thing

A small thing, really,
the way you caught yourself
slipping the postcard-cum-bookmark
upside down into a book of poems
written by a shy man of Orkney.

A keepsake postcard
brought home from a museum in Vienna
framing the soft glow of the crucified Christ
hewn from golden wood
against a background of medieval gloom.

An upside down crucified one was ancient Rome's
severest thumbs down.
You turned the card right-side up.
You won't let it happen in your home.
By such private gestures we become

known to ourselves. Even late in the day.
Out the window, afternoon darkens.
The pond is pitted with rain.
And you recall the old dream
about the way you meant to be.

Family Reunion Picnic
    Domine miserere nobis

You gaze upon the angelic precision of their sunlit faces,
  the familiar become dear.

Their choric voices and laughter weave a hymn
  you half-heard once drifting from a hill.

Now you understand: This is what you wanted.
  Those years of parched seeking lie far behind.

A white wafer moon floats high overhead.
  A warm breeze flows through the shoreline maples

and moves a lock of your baby grandson's sandy hair.
  The swimming tide is almost in.

There is still time for second helpings.
  Buoyed by tenderness, you rise into the air

to gaze down upon the mother of your wife.
  You call her name. Her face turns into the radiance.

And you ask: "Do you want a little more pie?"
Though "Dost thou" is what you mean.

At Last, the Sea

You ask me, stranger, what route I took
to arrive at the sea's steady interrogation.
I tell you almost anything
and leave out everything
about those I love.

When you say the windy blue sea
is magnificent I say nothing.
I rest my eye, instead, on the taut silence
of a blue flower in the sedge
moving in the sun.

Consider

I'm no buttonholer
on the subject
of my beautiful grandson,
nine months old.
I only ask you consider

just this once
how a mid-winter sun
on a weekday afternoon
lit a stream flashing
from the woods into the bay.

How the little boy in my arms
turned his head softly
as a down-drifting feather
when he heard the silver
vocables of quick water.

How his blue eyes rested there,
arrested by sunlit water
streaming over stones.
And how I looked down
into the stream twice

as I stepped over.
And carried him down
the corridor of time
towards a world told to us
through words.

While his silence gazed back
over my shoulder
at the world shining in silence
as it must have
the first day.

Mike Dillon lives in Indianola, Washington, a small town on Puget Sound northwest of Seattle, Washington. He is the author of five books of poetry and three books of haiku. Several of his haiku were included in *Haiku in English: The First Hundred Years*, from W.W. Norton (2013). His most recent full-length book is *Departures: Poetry and Prose on the Removal of Bainbridge Island's Japanese Americans After Pearl Harbor,* from Unsolicited Press (2019). American Book Award winner Anna Odessa Linzer wrote of *Departures*: "This collection finds me at a loss for words to describe the perfect beauty, the searing pain held in his words." Finishing Line Press published his chapbook, *The Return*, in 2021, which was reviewed by British editor and poet Matthew Paul in *The Sphinx* in the U.K., who noted Mike Dillon's "quiet, almost effortlessly-crafted poetry which asks deep questions."

www.ingramcontent.com/pod-product-compliance
Lightning Source LLC
Chambersburg PA
CBHW022128090426
42743CB00008B/1059